WALKING by FAITH

Five / The Sacraments

Assessment

Principal Program Consultants

Rev. Terry M. Odien, MA

Rev. Michael D. Place, STD

Dr. Addie Lorraine Walker, SSND

BROWN-ROA

A Division of Harcourt Brace & Company

BROWN-ROA
A Division of Harcourt Brace & Company

Our Mission

The primary mission of BROWN-ROA is to provide the Catholic and Christian markets with the highest quality catechetical print and media resources.
The content of these resources reflects the best insights of current theology, methodology, and pedagogical research.
The resources are practical and easy to use, designed to meet expressed market needs, and written to reflect the teachings of the Catholic Church.

The Ad Hoc Committee to Oversee the Use of the Catechism, National Conference of Catholic Bishops, has found this catechetical series to be in conformity with the *Catechism of the Catholic Church.*

Using the Assessments

This booklet contains reproducible masters for seven unit assessments as well as for a year-end assessment. Each assessment enables you to monitor the students' progress in areas including key ideas, religious knowledge and beliefs, and religious practices. Answer keys are provided. The year-end assessment also includes questions that allow the students to apply what they've learned in an open-ended format. Guidelines for evaluating the responses are provided, but you should always allow for individual differences in the responses. For additional guidance in working with the assessments, see the notes under Unit Checkpoint Review in the Teaching Guide.

The unit assessments cover material from the three content chapters as well as from the seasonal chapter. The unit assessment is best given after all four chapters in a unit have been explored, even if done so out of numerical sequence. If you have not covered all the material in a unit, you may wish to delete some of the questions from the master or use some of the questions as the basis of your own individualized assessment.

The year-end assessment is divided into two parts. Part one covers units one through four; part two covers units five through seven. Individual preference or local requirements may dictate that you give both a mid-year and an end-of-year assessment. If so, use parts one and two of the year-end assessment separately for this purpose.

Cover illustration by Kathy Petrauskas

Printed in the United States of America

ISBN 0-15-950525-9

10 9 8 7 6 5 4 3 2 1

Name ____ Date ______________

UNIT ONE ASSESSMENT

Creation Celebrates God's Love

Key Ideas

Match the terms in Column B with the meanings in Column A.

	Column A	Column B
______	1. All things seen and unseen	A. stewardship
______	2. God's plan for all creation	B. revelation
______	3. An act of disobedience toward God by the first humans	C. sin
______	4. The gradual process of coming to know God	D. creation
______	5. The immortal part of our being	E. doctrine
______	6. Responsible care for God's creation	F. providence
______	7. The opposite of God's good plan for creation	G. assumption
______	8. The formal teaching of the Church	H. evil
______	9. Our choice to turn away from God	I. soul
______	10. Mary was taken to heaven in body and soul	J. original sin

Religious Knowledge and Beliefs

*Write the letter of the choice that **best** completes the sentence or answers the question.*

______ 11. The authors of Genesis were ______, or prompted by the Holy Spirit.
A. scientific
B. not free
C. imaginative
D. inspired

______ 12. God created humans ______.
A. in his own image
B. before anything else
C. to take care of the garden
D. to keep the animals company

______ 13. One way God reveals his love to us is through ______.
A. nature
B. evil
C. original sin
D. pain and suffering

Name ____

UNIT ONE ASSESSMENT

_______ **14.** Evil is _______.

A. part of God's plan **B.** the result of original sin
C. the result of God's goodness **D.** created by God

_______ **15.** God gave us responsibility for _______.

A. getting possessions **B.** deciding the fate of others
C. caring for creation **D.** following our own desires

_______ **16.** God sent Jesus, his Son, into the world to _______.

A. carry out his plan for creation **B.** demonstrate his power
C. punish Jesus **D.** reward the faithful

_______ **17.** Why did Jesus tell the people not to worry?

A. He knew they could care for themselves. **B.** Because they believed in God's providence.
C. He knew life was safe in villages. **D.** Because God would provide for their needs.

_______ **18.** Catholics believe that Mary was _______.

A. the last person to see Jesus **B.** reunited with Jesus
C. a sinner **D.** the original creator

_______ **19.** The assumption of Mary is important because it _______.

A. proves the Bible is right **B.** shows God's love
C. gives hope that we can share in Christ's resurrection **D.** demonstrates the importance of obedience

Religious Practices

_______ **20.** All of the following show reverence for God's creation **except** _______.

A. respecting nature **B.** buying presents
C. loving others **D.** worshiping God

_______ **21.** To better understand Scripture, you should _______.

A. memorize every passage you read **B.** make up your own interpretation
C. skip any hard words that you don't understand **D.** reflect on what the passage means to you

_______ **22.** We show our trust in God by _______.

A. arguing with our parents **B.** wishing for happiness
C. helping others in need **D.** teasing our friends

Name ____

Unit One Assessment

_______ **23.** Which action is **not** good stewardship?
- **A.** Cathy feeds and walks her dog every day.
- **B.** Matt puts half of his allowance in the Sunday collection.
- **C.** Jimmy throws soda bottles into a stream.
- **D.** Rosa helps her grandmother with household chores.

_______ **24.** By making a donation at the presentation of the gifts we show _______.
- **A.** how wealthy we are
- **B.** our care for God's creation
- **C.** who needs the most help
- **D.** the importance of possessions

_______ **25.** Your image is determined by _______.
- **A.** what you wear
- **B.** what your friends think
- **C.** what you drink
- **D.** what you believe

Name ______________________________ Date ____________

UNIT TWO ASSESSMENT

We Worship Our God

Key Ideas

Match the terms in Column B with the meanings in Column A.

	Column A	Column B
________	1. Power that enables us to believe God is with us	A. Emmanuel
________	2. Everlasting, without end	B. faith
________	3. Lifting up our hearts and minds in love	C. grace
________	4. Make holy	D. immortal
________	5. Means "God is with us"	E. intercede
________	6. The gift of God's life in us	F. Mass
________	7. Offering public praise and thanks to God	G. prayer
________	8. Pray to God on another's behalf	H. prophet
________	9. Someone who speaks God's message to us	I. sanctify
________	10. A sacred meal of sacrifice and praise to God	J. worship

Religious Knowledge and Beliefs

*Write the letter of the choice that **best** completes the sentence or answers the question.*

________ 11. Catholics believe that true happiness is found in ________.

A. being popular with friends
B. having many gifts and talents
C. having a comfortable life
D. maintaining a close relationship with God

________ 12. At the Last Supper Jesus washed the feet of the apostles because he ________.

A. knew it was expected of him
B. wanted to show them how to serve others
C. knew they were rich and powerful
D. wanted to give them a sign of his holiness

________ 13. Jesus came into the world to ________.

A. be with his apostles
B. show God's love for everyone
C. practice his preaching skills
D. become famous as a "miracle worker"

Name ______________________________

UNIT TWO ASSESSMENT

______ **14.** Through the sacrament of Baptism, we receive the gift of
- **A.** faith
- **B.** prophecy
- **C.** sight
- **D.** healing

______ **15.** The official public worship of the Church is called ______.
- **A.** the Sabbath
- **B.** liturgy
- **C.** the Holy Trinity
- **D.** the Book of Prayer

______ **16.** The sacraments mostly serve as a means to ______.
- **A.** unite us with God and each other
- **B.** learn prayers by heart
- **C.** encourage others who have problems
- **D.** help us make decisions in our lives

______ **17.** What do we celebrate on Pentecost?
- **A.** the baptism of Jesus by John the Baptist
- **B.** Jesus washing the feet of his apostles
- **C.** the Holy Spirit coming to the apostles
- **D.** the preaching and healing ministry of Jesus

______ **18.** Canonization is the ceremony at which a person ______.
- **A.** becomes a priest
- **B.** is named a saint
- **C.** is baptized
- **D.** is confirmed

______ **19.** On November 1 we celebrate the Feast of ______.
- **A.** the Assumption
- **B.** the Ascension
- **C.** All Saints
- **D.** All Souls

Religious Practices

______ **20.** We should treat others with respect because ______.
- **A.** they may do us a favor sometime in the future
- **B.** we want to show that we have good manners
- **C.** we may be punished if we don't
- **D.** each person is made in the image of God

______ **21.** Meditation is a special type of prayer. When you meditate, you should ______.
- **A.** tell God all of your problems
- **B.** ask God to grant you many favors
- **C.** quietly listen to God with an open heart
- **D.** pray earnestly for your family and friends

______ **22.** We are **not** participating fully in the Mass when we ______.
- **A.** say the responses aloud
- **B.** join in singing the hymns
- **C.** listen to the readings
- **D.** watch our friends

Name ____________________

Unit Two Assessment

_______ **23.** The main purpose of participating in a prayer service is to _______.
A. get together with friends **B.** learn more about prayer and liturgy
C. use audiovisual aids **D.** worship God

_______ **24.** If we remember to use God's grace, we will _______.
A. be powerful and mighty **B.** have wealth and fame
C. grow in holiness **D.** do whatever we like

_______ **25.** When we pray a litany, we pray _______.
A. a series of short prayers **B.** the Pentecost song
C. words from a psalm **D.** the Rosary

Name ________________________________ Date ____________

UNIT THREE ASSESSMENT

Jesus Is a Sacrament

Key Ideas

Using the word bank below, fill in the blanks with the letters of the correct terms.

A. compassion	**B.** Messiah	**C.** redeemer
D. divine	**E.** miracles	**F.** repentance
G. incarnation	**H.** parables	**I.** resurrection
J. kingdom of God		

1. The _______ refers to the Son of God becoming man.
2. Turning away from sin and toward God is called _______.
3. Stories that teach a lesson are called _______.
4. Rising to new life as Jesus did is called _______.
5. One who is willing to suffer with another is said to have _______.
6. A _______ is one who saves others.
7. The name given to Christ, meaning God's Chosen One, is _______.
8. God's reign of justice, love, and peace is called the _______.
9. Physical signs of God's power and love are called _______.
10. The word _______ means "God-like."

Religious Knowledge and Beliefs

Write the letter of the choice that **best** *completes the sentence or answers the question.*

_______ **11.** The most perfect image of God is found in _______.

A. the paintings by Leonardo da Vinci
B. works of creation, such as the sun and moon
C. the words and actions of Jesus Christ
D. descriptive words used in the Bible

_______ **12.** A mystery, such as the incarnation, can be understood _______.

A. through Baptism
B. by using our senses
C. by attending Mass
D. only through faith

Name ____________________

Unit Three Assessment

_______ **13.** Catholics believe that Jesus is both God and human. We know this _______.

A. because our friends say it is true
B. because God has revealed this truth to us
C. by our natural reason
D. through our own sensory knowledge

_______ **14.** We are given the grace to be living images of God when we _______.

A. are born
B. go to religion class
C. celebrate the Eucharist
D. are baptized

_______ **15.** All of the following are features of Jesus' parables **except** _______.

A. opening with "The kingdom of heaven is like . . ."
B. use of animal instead of human characters
C. events from everyday life
D. surprise endings that make us think

_______ **16.** The treasures of God's kingdom are love, justice, and _______.

A. peace
B. power
C. wealth
D. fame

_______ **17.** Why did Jesus suffer and die on the cross?

A. He had preached against the Roman government.
B. He wanted to prove he had courage and wasn't afraid.
C. His apostles failed to save him.
D. He wanted to save us.

_______ **18.** The Paschal mystery means that Jesus _______.

A. came to earth in human form
B. performed wonderful miracles
C. suffered, died, and rose again to new life
D. often told short stories to make a point

_______ **19.** The season in which we prepare for the birth of Christ is called _______.

A. Lent
B. Pentecost
C. Advent
D. Ordinary Time

Religious Practices

_______ **20.** The best way we can reflect God's image is to _______.

A. try to become better educated
B. show that we care for others
C. baptize as many people as we can
D. attend Mass daily

Name ______________________________

Unit Three Assessment

______ **21.** We can best understand Jesus' parables when we read them ______.
A. aloud **B.** with other people
C. at the same time every day **D.** with a sense of wonder

______ **22.** People become modern-day miracle workers when they ______.
A. use their creativity **B.** work hard at their jobs
C. become rich and famous **D.** serve God in word and deed

______ **23.** An example of a work of mercy is ______.
A. studying for a test **B.** cleaning your home
C. learning a new skill **D.** praying for the dead

______ **24.** The most perfect way to celebrate the Paschal mystery is to ______.
A. celebrate the Sacrament of Confirmation **B.** celebrate the Eucharist
C. pray for our friends and family **D.** attend Mass on Christmas

______ **25.** An important way to prepare for the coming of Jesus at Christmas is to ______.
A. make a list of what we want for Christmas **B.** celebrate the Sacrament of Reconciliation
C. receive ashes on our forehead **D.** carry palm branches in a procession

Name ______________________________ Date ____________

UNIT FOUR ASSESSMENT

The Church Is a Sacrament

Key Ideas

Using the word bank below, fill in the blanks with the letters of the correct terms.

A. chrism	B. hospitality	C. magi
D. contemplative	E. infallible	F. sponsor
G. elect	H. magisterium	I. vocation
J. fidelity		

1. _______ is the gift of caring for the needs of a guest.
2. The pronouncements of the pope and bishops are called the teaching authority of the Church, or _______.
3. Catholics believe that some of the Church's teachings are _______, or free from error.
4. A person who helps someone preparing to be a Catholic on his or her faith journey is called a _______.
5. Those chosen to enter into full membership with the Church are called the _______.
6. The holy oil used in Confirmation is called _______.
7. Being faithful in keeping one's promises is called _______.
8. Wise men from the East, the _______, followed a star to Bethlehem.
9. A call from God to serve him and others is a _______.
10. One who has dedicated his or her life to prayer and work apart from the world is a member of a _______ religious community.

Religious Knowledge and Beliefs

Write the letter of the choice that **best** *completes the sentence or answers the question.*

_______ 11. One, holy, catholic, and apostolic are _______.
A. practices of the Church
B. symbols of the Church
C. beliefs of the Church
D. marks of the Church

Name ______________________________

Unit Four Assessment

_______ **12.** When we say that the Church is apostolic, we mean _______.
A. it is named after the apostles
B. the Church was built on the apostles' efforts
C. the apostles were present at Christ's birth
D. the apostles recognized Christ as the Messiah right away

_______ **13.** When we share our faith with others, our message needs to be *authentic*. This statement means _______.
A. our message must be faithful to the word of God
B. all people must believe the teachings
C. the teachings must be reasonable
D. the teachings must have been proven by science

_______ **14.** The image of the Church as Body of Christ refers to the fact that the people _______.
A. are pilgrims going to their true home in heaven
B. believe in all God's promises
C. rely on the pope and the bishops
D. though many, are united in one Church under Christ

_______ **15.** Concupiscence is _______.
A. falling under the spell of Cupid
B. believing everything the Church teaches
C. the desire to be the best we can be
D. the tendency to turn away from God

_______ **16.** The process of becoming a member of the Church is called _______.
A. vocation
B. election
C. initiation
D. immersion

_______ **17.** The catechumenate is a period of _______.
A. exams and tests
B. finding a partner
C. growing in faith
D. celebrating the sacraments

_______ **18.** Conversion is _______.
A. bread and wine becoming the Body and Blood of Christ
B. the lifelong process of turning toward God
C. praying for other people
D. receiving the Eucharist at the Easter Vigil Mass

_______ **19.** In the Sacrament of Matrimony, people make sacred promises called _______.
A. prayers
B. conversions
C. vows
D. blessings

Name ______________________________

Unit Four Assessment

_______ **20.** The evangelical counsels are _______.
A. the writings of the four evangelists
B. vows of poverty, chastity, and obedience made by members of religious communities
C. large meetings of church leaders
D. advice given to engaged couples

_______ **21.** The Feast of the Epiphany celebrates the manifestation of _______.
A. Mary
B. Matthew
C. Cana
D. Jesus

Religious Practices

_______ **22.** Because the Church is one, we should _______.
A. ignore those who are not Catholic
B. avoid those who are not Christian
C. respect the beliefs of other Christians
D. join another Christian religion

_______ **23.** Every year in late January in the United States, a week is set aside to pray _______.
A. that the Church will be holy even as Christ is holy
B. that all Christians will be united in one Church
C. that Christ will send the apostles back to our world
D. that the end of the world will come soon

_______ **24.** When Christ says that we cannot enter God's kingdom unless we are born again of water and the spirit, he means that everyone should _______.
A. be baptized
B. be confirmed
C. receive the Eucharist
D. die and return to this life

_______ **25.** One way to answer God's call is to _______.
A. ignore the needs of others
B. argue with your family
C. care only about yourself
D. use your talents wisely

Name ______________________________ Date ______________

UNIT FIVE ASSESSMENT

The Life of Grace

Key Ideas

Match the terms in Column B with the meanings in Column A.

	Column A	Column B
______	1. The way we think about ourselves and our experiences	A. fortitude
		B. Beatitudes
______	2. 40-day season of preparation for Easter	C. attitude
______	3. A constant, firm choice to do good	D. justice
______	4. Helps us act with courage to do what is right	E. Lent
______	5. Making sure all people have their due as God's children	F. morality
______	6. *Philosophy* means love of this virtue	G. prudence
______	7. The way we act based on what we believe is right and wrong	H. temperance
		I. virtue
______	8. The virtue of keeping all things in good balance	J. wisdom
______	9. Jesus' teachings about blessedness	
______	10. Virtue of good judgment in action	

Religious Knowledge and Beliefs

Write the letter of the choice that **best** *completes the sentence or answers the question.*

______ 11. In the Sermon on the Mount, Jesus teaches that true happiness can be found only in seeking ______.

A. money
B. popularity
C. righteousness
D. friendship

______ 12. Which of the following statements **best** summarizes the Beatitudes?

A. God wants us to treat others the way they treat us.
B. God wants everyone to have many problems in this world.
C. God expects those with many problems in this world to sit and pity themselves.
D. God will reward those who act in a loving way toward others.

Name ____________________

UNIT FIVE ASSESSMENT

_______ 13. An action is morally good if _______.
A. our friends agree to it
B. our parents say it is
C. it is in agreement with the Church's teachings
D. it does not break any laws of the United States

_______ 14. The four cardinal virtues are prudence, justice, fortitude, and _______.
A. wisdom
B. honesty
C. conscience
D. temperance

_______ 15. Contrition involves all of the following **except** _______.
A. expressing sorrow for sin
B. asking God for forgiveness
C. resolving not to sin again
D. making public penance

_______ 16. The purpose of the Sacrament of Anointing of the Sick is to _______.
A. bless someone who is dying
B. give medicine to someone who is sick
C. offer the healing touch of Christ to an ill or suffering person
D. forgive someone who has sinned

Religious Practices

_______ 17. When making a moral decision, you should _______.
A. consult an encyclopedia
B. listen only to your feelings
C. listen to your conscience and pray
D. let your friends decide for you

_______ 18. Which Beatitude are you practicing when you forgive your friend for doing something bad to you?
A. Blessed are the merciful . . .
B. Blessed are the meek . . .
C. Blessed are the poor in spirit . . .
D. Blessed are the clean of heart . . .

_______ 19. You are practicing the Beatitude "Blessed are the meek . . ." when your friend is telling you about winning a swim meet and you _______.
A. interrupt to tell him about a home run you have made
B. act bored with his story
C. praise him for his success
D. tell him you have to go home now

_______ 20. Sarah's favorite TV program begins at 8:30, but she has an English test tomorrow. She decides to skip the program and study an extra half hour. She practices the virtue of _______.
A. prudence
B. justice
C. temperance
D. fortitude

Name ____________________

Unit Five Assessment

_______ **21.** LaShanda's younger sister had helped her fold the laundry. When Mother gave LaShanda $.50, she immediately handed a quarter to her sister saying, "Keesha helped, too!" LaShanda was practicing the virtue of ______.

A. prudence
B. justice
C. temperance
D. fortitude

_______ **22.** When Chad sees an older, popular student take Tim's lunch, he threatens to report him if the lunch isn't put back unopened right away. Chad is practicing the virtue of ______.

A. prudence
B. justice
C. temperance
D. fortitude

_______ **23.** One of the first steps you take in celebrating the Sacrament of Reconciliation is to ______.

A. confess your sins to the priest
B. anoint another person
C. receive Holy Communion
D. receive absolution

_______ **24.** A person recovering from a heart attack is **most** likely to celebrate the Sacrament of ______.

A. Baptism
B. Reconciliation
C. Matrimony
D. Anointing of the Sick

_______ **25.** During the Lenten Season you should ______.

A. celebrate with a feast each day
B. splurge by buying new clothes
C. look into your heart and do penance willingly
D. be baptized

Name ______________________________ Date ____________

UNIT SIX ASSESSMENT

The Eucharist, Our Great Sacrament

Key Ideas

Use the letters of the terms in each box to complete the sentences below.

A. assemble	B. obligation	C. presides	D. sacred	E. Tradition

When people come together to honor God, the gathering is **(1)** _______ . Our ancestors in faith read the Scriptures and handed down their understanding of God's word, which is called **(2)** _______ . It is our **(3)** _______ to come together as a community to worship. When we **(4)** _______ for the Eucharist, a bishop or priest **(5)** _______ over the gathering.

A. hymn	B. Liturgy of the Word	C. Liturgy of the Eucharist	D. Blessed Sacrament	E. tabernacle

The Introductory Rites begin with a **(6)** _______ sung to praise God. During the **(7)** _______ there are readings and a homily. During the **(8)** _______ we receive Holy Communion. Any leftover consecrated hosts are kept in a chest or container called a **(9)** _______ . Jesus is truly present in the **(10)** _______ .

Religious Knowledge and Beliefs

Write the letter of the choice that ***best*** *completes the sentence or answers the question.*

_______ **11.** The faith community has been called the Body of Christ. Which statement best explains how the members of the community are like the parts of a body?

A. Each person is necessary and brings unique gifts to the community.
B. All of the people are united and feel close to one another.
C. All of the people love Christ and often receive his Body.
D. Each of the members has a body.

Name ____

Unit Six Assessment

_______ **12.** An ordained minister, as head of the Eucharistic assembly, is acting in the person of _______.

A. Christ **B.** a bishop
C. a priest **D.** each of us

_______ **13.** A hymn is a _______.

A. prayer to the Holy Spirit **B.** gesture used by the priest
C. Latin word meaning God **D.** sacred song

_______ **14.** In the book of Scripture readings used in the liturgy, the readings are repeated every _______.

A. year **B.** two years
C. three years **D.** four years

_______ **15.** Both the Old Testament and the New Testament tell about _______.

A. Marcion **B.** the apostles
C. Jesus Christ **D.** the same God

_______ **16.** Which of these is part of the Introductory Rite?

A. general intercessions **B.** the Creed
C. the consecration **D.** the penitential rite

_______ **17.** Which of the following sets of readings is most likely to have a common theme?

A. the responsorial psalm and the second reading **B.** the first reading and the gospel
C. the second reading and the gospel **D.** the first reading and the second reading

_______ **18.** During which part of the Mass does the bishop, priest, or deacon explain what the word of God means in our lives?

A. the homily **B.** the greeting
C. the penitential rite **D.** the responsorial psalm

_______ **19.** The Communion Rite begins with _______.

A. the Eucharistic Prayer **B.** the Lord's Prayer
C. the Preface **D.** Holy Communion

_______ **20.** The bread and wine become the Body and Blood of Christ when they are _______.

A. distributed to the community **B.** eaten and drunk by the community
C. consecrated through the power of the Holy Spirit **D.** stored in a tabernacle

Name ____

Unit Six Assessment

_______ 21. The Triduum includes ______.

A. Palm Sunday and Holy Thursday, and Holy Saturday

B. Palm Sunday, Holy Thursday, and Good Friday

C. Holy Thursday, Good Friday, and Holy Saturday

D. Ash Wednesday, Palm Sunday, and Easter

Religious Practices

_______ 22. All of these are ways to make Mass more real to you **except** ______.

A. actively participating

B. coming early to look over the readings

C. using the time to plan the coming week

D. inviting relatives and friends to join you

_______ 23. Which of the following is the **most** important reason for listening to the readings carefully?

A. God is present in his word.

B. The readings all express the theme of the day.

C. The readings show how God punishes sinners.

D. The readings are the only parts of the Mass that change from week to week.

_______ 24. During the Liturgy of the Word, we trace a cross on our foreheads, lips, and hearts to show respect for ______.

A. ourselves

B. each other

C. the gospel

D. the priest

_______ 25. The **most** important reason for receiving Communion often is to ______.

A. stay connected to the Church

B. temporarily forget our daily lives

C. participate in worship with our friends

D. be transformed and joined in the Body and Blood of Christ

Name ______________________________ Date ____________

UNIT SEVEN ASSESSMENT

The Paschal Mystery

Key Ideas

Match the terms in Column B with the meanings in Column A.

Column A

_____ 1. Rituals to help us move from our earthly life to life with God

_____ 2. The word of God that forms part of worship for both Jews and Christians

_____ 3. Any form of hatred directed against Jewish people

_____ 4. Israelites' journey from slavery in Egypt to freedom

_____ 5. "Food for the journey" from death to life

_____ 6. Keeping watch by night

_____ 7. White cloth laid over a coffin

_____ 8. John's vision of heaven

_____ 9. Special meal with which the Jewish people celebrate Passover

_____ 10. We celebrate the sacraments to remind us of this

Column B

A. anti-Semitism

B. Exodus

C. God's reign

D. new Jerusalem

E. Old Testament

F. pall

G. Seder

H. viaticum

I. vigil

J. last rites

Religious Knowledge and Beliefs

Write the letter of the choice that **best** *completes the sentence or answers the question.*

_____ 11. Jews and Christians both share all the following **except** _____.

A. the Ten Commandments
B. the Eucharist
C. a covenant with God
D. the Old Testament

_____ 12. The feast of the Passover celebrates the passing of _____.

A. God's Spirit over the waters of creation
B. another year
C. Christ into heaven
D. the Israelites from slavery to freedom

Name ______________________________

UNIT SEVEN ASSESSMENT

_______ 13. The holiest day of the year among Jews is the day of atonement, or _______.

A. Sukkot
B. Yom Kippur
C. Shavu'ot
D. Rosh Hashanah

_______ 14. The eight-day festival of lights, celebrating the return of the Jews' freedom to worship after the destruction of the Temple in Jerusalem, is _______.

A. Rosh Hashanah
B. Yom Kippur
C. Sukkot
D. Hanukkah

_______ 15. How did the Apostle Paul respond to early Christians who did not believe in resurrection?

A. He used reason and logic to prove their views wrong.
B. He told them, "Let us eat and drink, for tomorrow we die."
C. He forgave them their sins.
D. He told them the Christian faith was in vain.

_______ 16. We can participate in the mystery of Christ's resurrection through _______.

A. the feast of Sukkot
B. the Passover Seder
C. reading the Old Testament
D. the sacraments

_______ 17. The last rites include the _______.

A. Sacrament of Reconciliation
B. Easter Vigil
C. lighting of the Hanukkah candles
D. retelling of the story of Exodus

_______ 18. When Christ returns at the end of time, which will remain?

A. signs
B. love
C. sacraments
D. symbols

_______ 19. John saw a vision of a holy city, the new _______.

A. Egypt
B. Rome
C. Jerusalem
D. Nazareth

Religious Practices

_______ 20. To better understand the Jewish people and their religion, you should read _______.

A. the Old Testament
B. Corinthians
C. Revelation
D. the Book of Life

Name ____

UNIT SEVEN ASSESSMENT

_______ **21.** Which of the following statements about the Seder and the Mass on Holy Thursday is incorrect?

A. Both recall an event that happened long ago.
B. Both are sacred meals that God commanded.
C. Both are celebrated in a place of community worship.
D. Both follow a specific ritual.

_______ **22.** When someone close to us dies, we may react in many ways, but we should **not** _______.

A. pray
B. ask questions
C. feel confused
D. turn away from God

_______ **23.** An example of a work of mercy is helping _______.

A. our friends
B. ourselves
C. people in need
D. our parents

_______ **24.** Which of these is a work of mercy?

A. reading a book
B. singing a song
C. watching a sunrise
D. visiting a person who is sick

_______ **25.** When it comes to doing the work of God's kingdom, we are all _______.

A. like the monkeys who see, hear, and speak no evil
B. just beginners
C. like accomplished musicians
D. like angels in heaven

Name ____ Date ____________

YEAR-END ASSESSMENT **Part 1**

Key Ideas

Use the letters of the terms in each box to complete the sentences below.

A. Genesis	B. image of God	C. inspired	D. pray	E. providence

Two stories of creation are told in the Book of **(1)** _______ . The people who wrote these stories and all of the other stories in the Bible were **(2)** _______ by the Holy Spirit. When we read the Bible, we learn about God's **(3)** _______ , his loving and caring plan for all creation. Part of God's plan was to send Jesus, the perfect **(4)** _______ , into our world. When we **(5)** _______ , or lift up our hearts and minds to God in love, we imitate Jesus.

A. kingdom of God	B. parables	C. conversion	D. miracles	E. repent

Jesus called people to **(6)** _______ , or turn away from sin. He knew **(7)** _______ was a lifelong process of turning toward God. He performed many **(8)** _______ . The **(9)** _______ that he told teach us about the **(10)** _______ , God's reign of love, justice, and peace.

Religious Knowledge and Beliefs

Write the letter of the choice that **best** *completes the sentence or answers the question.*

_______ **11.** Evil is a result of _______.
- **A.** God's plan for the world
- **B.** sin
- **C.** death
- **D.** suffering

_______ **12.** The Feast of the Assumption celebrates the fact that Mary _______.
- **A.** has always been free from sin
- **B.** is the Mother of God
- **C.** was taken into heaven, body and soul
- **D.** is queen of heaven

_______ **13.** The power that enables us to believe in and respond to God is _______.
- **A.** faith
- **B.** holiness
- **C.** our good actions
- **D.** love

Name ______________________________

Year-End Assessment

______ 14. The gift of God's own life that helps us become more like God is called ______.
A. creation B. humanity
C. devotion D. grace

Below are three mysteries that Catholics believe. State what you know about each.

15. The Holy Trinity means

____

____

16. The incarnation means

____

____

17. The Paschal mystery celebrates

____

____

Religious Practices

______ 18. At the end of the Mass, we are sent out to ______.
A. pray our private prayers B. read the Bible at home
C. serve God's people D. enjoy our friends

______ 19. We reflect God's presence in our world most perfectly when we ______.
A. write prayers B. care for others
C. look for pictures of Jesus in books D. imagine God's image

______ 20. A good example of a work of mercy is ______.
A. practicing soccer skills B. finishing my homework
C. visiting a friend who is sick D. reading the Bible

______ 21. We answer God's call when we ______.
A. worry about our appearance B. follow the popular crowd
C. care only about winning D. serve others

Name ______________________________

YEAR-END ASSESSMENT

Explain the importance of the following actions or words of Jesus. What point was he making?

22. Jesus washed the feet of his apostles the evening of the Last Supper.

____

____

23. Jesus said, "You are Peter, and upon this rock I will build my Church."

____

____

Name ______________________________ Date ____________

YEAR-END ASSESSMENT **Part 2**

Key Ideas

Match the terms in Column B with the meanings in Column A.

	Column A	Column B
______	**1.** Our gift from God that guides us in choosing what is good	**A.** Beatitudes
______	**2.** A constant, firm choice to do good	**B.** Blessed Sacrament
______	**3.** Sayings of Jesus that point the way to true happiness	**C.** conscience
______	**4.** The understanding of Scripture passed on to each generation of Christians	**D.** covenant
______	**5.** The Eucharistic bread	**E.** conversion
______	**6.** God's sacred bond with us	**F.** Exodus
______	**7.** Turning to God in Christ	**G.** last rites
______	**8.** The Israelites' journey from slavery in Egypt to freedom	**H.** Tradition
______	**9.** Rituals to help us pass over from death to life with God	**I.** viaticum
______	**10.** Last Eucharist; food for the journey	**J.** virtue

Name ____________________

Year-End Assessment

Religious Knowledge and Beliefs

*Write the letter of the choice that **best** completes the sentence or answers the question.*

_______ **11.** The two main parts of the Mass are the Liturgy of the Word and the _______.

A. Liturgy of the Eucharist
B. Introductory Rite
C. Penitential Rite
D. Presentation of the Gifts

_______ **12.** The bread and wine become the Body and Blood of Jesus during the _______.

A. Doxology
B. words of consecration
C. Seder
D. Sacrament of Baptism

_______ **13.** At Passover Jews all over the world remember the time when God _______.

A. gave the Ten Commandments
B. created the universe
C. led the Israelites from slavery in Egypt
D. caused the harvest to be great

_______ **14.** At the Easter Vigil we give thanks to God for _______.

A. our food and shelter
B. family and friends
C. Christ's victory over death
D. the beauty of creation

State what you know about each term below.

15. What are the four cardinal virtues?

____

____

16. What are the Sacraments of Healing?

____

____

17. What does anti-Semitism mean?

____

____

____

Name ____

Year-End Assessment

Religious Practices

_______ **18.** Which Beatitude am I practicing when I tell a friend I am sorry after a quarrel?

A. Blessed are the poor in spirit . . .
B. Blessed are they who mourn . . .
C. Blessed are the peacemakers . . .
D. Blessed are the clean of heart . . .

_______ **19.** When I finish all my homework before I play a video game, I practice the virtue of _______.

A. justice
B. prudence
C. temperance
D. fortitude

_______ **20.** We participate **best** during the Liturgy of the Word by _______.

A. being quiet during the readings
B. looking attentively at the reader
C. listening with our hearts and minds
D. sitting up straight

_______ **21.** I perform a work of mercy when I _______.

A. attend Mass
B. contribute to a food drive
C. do my homework
D. make my bed

Essay

Answer each question below.

22. Explain what Paul meant when he said, "If for this life only we have hoped in Christ, we are the most pitiable people of all."

____

____

____

____

23. Explain what Catholics and the Jewish people have in common.

____

____

____

____

Assessment Answer Key

Unit One

Key Ideas

1. D—creation
2. F—providence
3. J—original sin
4. B—revelation
5. I—soul
6. A—stewardship
7. H—evil
8. E—doctrine
9. C—sin
10. G—assumption

Religious Knowledge and Beliefs

11. D
12. A
13. A
14. B
15. C
16. A
17. D
18. B
19. C

Religious Practices

20. B
21. D
22. C
23. C
24. B
25. D

Unit Two

Key Ideas

1. B—faith
2. D—immortal
3. G—prayer
4. I—sanctify
5. A—Emmanuel
6. C—grace
7. J—worship
8. E—intercede
9. H—prophet
10. F—Mass

Religious Knowledge and Beliefs

11. D
12. B
13. B
14. A
15. B
16. A
17. C
18. B
19. C

Religious Practices

20. D
21. C
22. D
23. D
24. C
25. A

Unit Three

Key Ideas

1. G—incarnation
2. F—repentance
3. H—parables
4. I—resurrection
5. A—compassion
6. C—redeemer
7. B—Messiah
8. J—kingdom of God
9. E—miracles
10. D—divine

Religious Knowledge and Beliefs

11. C
12. D
13. B
14. D
15. B
16. A
17. D
18. C
19. C

Religious Practices

20. B
21. D
22. D
23. D
24. B
25. B

Assessment Answer Key

Unit Four

Key Ideas

1. B—hospitality
2. H—magisterium
3. E—infallible
4. F—sponsor
5. G—elect
6. A—chrism
7. J—fidelity
8. C—magi
9. I—vocation
10. D—contemplative

Religious Knowledge and Beliefs

11. D
12. B
13. A
14. D
15. D
16. C
17. C
18. B
19. C
20. B
21. D

Religious Practices

22. C
23. B
24. A
25. D

Unit Five

Key Ideas

1. C—attitude
2. E—Lent
3. I—virtue
4. A—fortitude
5. D—justice
6. J—wisdom
7. F—morality
8. H—temperance
9. B—Beatitudes
10. G—prudence

Religious Knowledge and Beliefs

11. C
12. D
13. C
14. D
15. D
16. C

Religious Practices

17. C
18. A
19. C
20. A
21. B
22. D
23. A
24. D
25. C

Unit Six

Key Ideas

1. D—sacred
2. E—Tradition
3. B—obligation
4. A—assemble
5. C—presides
6. A—hymn
7. B—Liturgy of the Word
8. C—Liturgy of the Eucharist
9. E—tabernacle
10. D—Blessed Sacrament

Religious Knowledge and Beliefs

11. A
12. A
13. D
14. C
15. D
16. D
17. B
18. A
19. B
20. C
21. C

Assessment Answer Key

Religious Practices
22. C
23. A
24. C
25. D

Unit Seven
Key Ideas
1. J—last rites
2. E—Old Testament
3. A—anti-Semitism
4. B—Exodus
5. H—viaticum
6. I—vigil
7. F—pall
8. D—new Jerusalem
9. G—Seder
10. C—God's reign

Religious Knowledge and Beliefs
11. B
12. D
13. B
14. D
15. A
16. D
17. A
18. B
19. C

Religious Practices
20. A
21. C
22. D
23. C
24. D
25. B

Year-End Assessment Answer Key

Part 1
Key Ideas
1. A—Genesis
2. C—inspired
3. E—providence
4. B—image of God
5. D—pray
6. E—repent
7. C—conversion
8. D—miracles
9. B—parables
10. A—kingdom of God

Religious Knowledge and Beliefs
11. B
12. C
13. A
14. D
15. Holy Trinity means there are three Persons in one God: God the Father, God the Son, and God the Holy Spirit.
16. The incarnation means the Son of God became human.
17. This mystery celebrates Jesus' life, death, and resurrection or his dying and rising to new life.

Religious Practices
18. C
19. B
20. C
21. D

General Scoring Guidelines for Items 22-23
2 points: The response is correct, thoughtful, and complete.
1 point: The response is partially correct but simplistic or shallow.
0 points: The response is incorrect or incomplete.
22. Examples:
 2 Jesus washed his friends' feet, even though servants usually did that only for rich guests. Jesus did that to show his friends that they must honor others as he honored them.
 1 Jesus washed the feet of the apostles to make them feel special.
 0 People had to wash their feet before supper.

YEAR-END ASSESSMENT ANSWER KEY

23. Examples:
    - 2 Peter knew that Jesus was the Son of God. Only God could have shown Peter that. So Jesus made Peter the foundation for his Church and turned over his ministry to Peter and the apostles.
    - 1 Peter knew that Jesus was the Son of God but the other apostles didn't.
    - 0 Peter showed Jesus a rock he could build the Church on.

Part 2

Key Ideas

1. C—conscience
2. J—virtue
3. A—Beatitudes
4. H—Tradition
5. B—Blessed Sacrament
6. D—covenant
7. E—conversion
8. F—Exodus
9. G—last rites
10. I—viaticum

Religious Knowledge and Beliefs

11. A
12. B
13. C
14. C
15. The four cardinal virtues are prudence, justice, fortitude, and temperance.
16. The Sacraments of Healing are Reconciliation and the Anointing of the Sick.
17. Anti-Semitism is any form of hatred directed toward the Jewish people.

Religious Practices

18. C
19. B
20. C
21. B

General Scoring Guidelines for Items 22-23

2 points: The response is correct, thoughtful, and complete.

1 point: The response is partially correct but simplistic or shallow.

0 points: The response is incorrect or incomplete.

22. Examples:
    - 2 Paul meant that Christians believe that Christ died for our sins and rose again so we could be saved. We know death is not all there is, and life has meaning.
    - 1 Paul meant it would be sad if this is the only life we get.
    - 0 You should have pity on other people worse off than you.
23. Examples:
    - 2 We have a lot in common with the Jewish people because we share a lot of the same ideas. We share the Ten Commandments, we read the Old Testament, and we believe in one God.
    - 1 We both believe in the same God.
    - 0 We live in the same country.